THE AXOLOTL FACT BOOK

Axolotls are special Mexican salamanders that never grow up. They stay forever young!

1

2 these adorable creatures are often referred to as "Mexican walking fish."

Axolotls are native to Xochimilco, a network of lakes and canals near Mexico City.

3

4 these amphibians are part of the axolotl salamander family, Ambystomatidae.

5 their lifespan can range from 10 to 15 years or more in captivity.

6 Axolotls can reach lengths of up to 12 inches (30 centimeters) or more.

7 the axolotl's name comes from the Nahuatl language, where "atl" means water, and "xolotl" refers to a deity.

8 Axolotls are related to other salamanders like the tiger salamander and the spotted salamander.

9

Axolotls have three hearts: two branchial hearts and one systemic heart to pump blood through their bodies.

10

In some places, there are dedicated rescue centers and conservation efforts to protect these incredible creatures.

11 Axolotls are excellent pets, especially for kids, as they are low-maintenance.

12 They prefer cool water temperatures, typically around 60-70°F (15-20°C).

13 Their glowing gills serve as natural nightlights, creating a magical ambiance in the dark.

14 Axolotls might not have teeth, but they have sharp ridges in their mouths to help grip prey.

15 No other animal can regrow body parts as efficiently as axolotls can.

16 These amphibians are very gentle and don't bite humans.

these creatures have their very own holiday! World Axolotl Day is celebrated on February 14th.

17

18

they are known to yawn, which helps them take in more oxygen.

In the wild, axolotls are critically endangered due to habitat loss and pollution.

19

20

Axolotl babies are called "larvae," and they often stick together in groups.

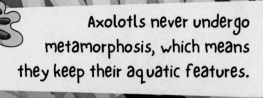

Axolotls never undergo metamorphosis, which means they keep their aquatic features.

21

22 When axolotls crawl on land, they have a wiggly walk that's just too cute.

23 Axolotls have been around for a very long time, even before the dinosaurs!

24 Females lay eggs, and males release sperm to fertilize them in the water.

25 Axolotls have a third eye called the parietal eye, and it helps them sense light and dark.

26

Axolotls are known to be excellent climbers, and they might surprise you by crawling up the sides of their tank.

27

Axolotls have amazing regenerative abilities; they can regrow limbs, spinal cord, heart, and even parts of their brain!

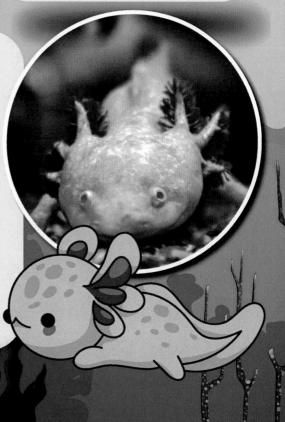

28 Their skin has a layer of mucus that helps protect them from the sun's rays.

29 Axolotls are incredibly patient hunters, waiting for prey to come to them.

30 When they want to move quickly, they can be speedy swimmers.

31 these creatures are a symbol of resilience and adaptability.

32 the axolotl is an important figure in Mexican folklore and mythology.

33 Axolotls are incredibly curious and will often investigate their surroundings.

they have an intricate courtship dance that involves touching and wiggling their tails. **34**

35 Axolotls are not picky eaters and will eat a variety of foods in captivity.

Some axolotls are born without eyes, but they can still get around using their other senses. **36**

37 they have a distinct dorsal fin that runs along their back.

they have tiny eardrums that are hidden behind their eyes to listen for sounds in the water. **38**

39 these creatures are incredibly photogenic and make great subjects for photography.

40 Axolotls can become overweight if they eat too much, just like people.

41 they can remain in a state of hibernation to conserve energy during periods of scarcity or adverse conditions.

42 Axolotls can travel long distances in search of food, mates, and new homes.

43

they can find their way home even if you move them to a new place; they're like little water wizards with GPS.

44

Axolotls can detect changes in water quality, making them great environmental indicators.

45 they use suction to capture prey in their mouths quickly.

46 Axolotls can live longer in captivity than in the wild due to better living conditions.

47 they can sometimes develop unusual colors and patterns in captivity.

48 Axolotls are often mistaken for fish because of their aquatic lifestyle.

49 Axolotls can lay hundreds of eggs during mating season.

50 they leave unique patterns on the bottom of their homes, almost like artwork.

Axolotls are among the most unique and fascinating animals in the world! **51**

52 these aquatic salamanders have no eyelids and can't close their eyes.

their DNA is incredibly complex and has intrigued scientists for years. **53**

54 Axolotls have long, feathery gills that help them extract oxygen from the water.

these amazing creatures can live at high altitudes, adapting to lower oxygen levels. **55**

56 Axolotls can move their eyes independently, watching out for both food and danger.

57 their skin secretes a protective slime to keep them safe from infections.

58 they show affection by gently nuzzling each other or even swimming in pairs.

59 Some axolotls are known to venture out of the water onto land for short periods.

60

Axolotls have a distinctive breathing behavior called "pumping," which helps them circulate oxygen-rich water.

61

these little architects build their homes by rearranging rocks and plants in their watery world.

62 Axolotls are highly sought after for scientific research in the fields of regenerative medicine and genetics.

63 They have a unique method of shedding their skin by eating it, leaving no waste behind.

64 When they hunt in groups, they coordinate their attacks with impressive precision.

65 Unlike many amphibians, they are completely aquatic and never leave the water.

66 Axolotls are cold-blooded, which means their body temperature depends on their environment.

67 Families of axolotls often stay together, creating strong bonds in their communities.

they have taste buds all over their bodies, so they can "taste" the water around them. **68**

69 they're experts at imitating the appearance of poisonous newts, which helps keep predators away.

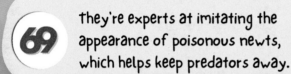

Axolotls have been featured in video games and literature, making them famous in popular culture. **70**

71 they are incredibly docile and rarely exhibit aggressive behavior.

they can stay incredibly still for long periods while hunting, making them excellent hunters. **72**

73 Axolotls have four toes on their front limbs and five toes on their hind limbs.

74 Their natural habitat, the Xochimilco canals, faces environmental threats from pollution and urban development.

75 Axolotls produce unique sounds, like clicks and chirps, to communicate with one another.

76 They can move silently through the water, making them expert spies in their underwater world.

77

they build nests from underwater plants and lay their eggs in them, protecting the future generation.

78

they build nests from underwater plants and lay their eggs in them, protecting the future generation.

79 they are often considered a "living fossil" due to their ancient evolutionary lineage.

80 Axolotls are quite sensitive to water quality, and regular water changes are essential for their health.

81 their metabolism slows down in cooler water, which can extend their lifespan.

82 Axolotls use a combination of smell and electroreception to locate prey.

83 In captivity, they should be provided with hides or caves for privacy and security.

84 these creatures are masters of adapting to their surroundings, changing color and shape as needed.

One of their unique features is the external gills that stick out from the sides of their heads. **85**

86 Axolotls are a crucial part of the ecosystem, helping control insect and small fish populations.

Axolotls can differentiate between different types of prey, helping them make effective hunting decisions. **87**

88 these amphibians have a peaceful demeanor and get along well with their tankmates.

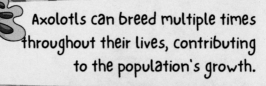

Axolotls can breed multiple times throughout their lives, contributing to the population's growth. **89**

90 Axolotls are the largest amphibians in the world, growing even bigger than some people's hands.

91 Axolotls have complex brains, allowing them to process a lot of information about their environment.

92 The axolotl's heart beats slowly, with a rate of about 20-30 beats per minute.

93 These creatures can regrow their jaws, which is especially impressive given their anatomy.

94

Some axolotls have been known to help injured tank mates by nuzzling and tending to their wounds.

95

they have been bred for research in labs worldwide, contributing to scientific discoveries.

96 These gentle creatures are rarely seen in the wild today due to their critically endangered status.

97 Axolotls have a unique "smell" that some describe as earthy or like the scent of cucumber.

98 Axolotls can live peacefully with other aquatic animals, such as fish and snails.

99 In the wild, axolotls serve as both predator and prey in the complex aquatic food web.

100 They occasionally weave aquatic plants into their skin, almost like wearing underwater clothing.

101 Axolotls are sensitive to water currents and prefer slow-moving water in their tanks.

In the wild, axolotls are known to ambush their prey with swift lunges and precise strikes. **102**

103 They have a high resistance to cancer, which makes them valuable in cancer research.

Axolotls are popular characters in Japanese manga and anime, adding to their global appeal. **104**

105 The axolotl's unusual appearance has led to its inclusion in art installations and public exhibitions.

Axolotls can be found in a variety of colors, including olive, golden, and even pink! **106**

107 In ancient Aztec culture, axolotls were considered a delicacy and a symbol of vitality and energy.

108 Axolotls are social animals, but they prefer to live alone in captivity to avoid stress.

109 In the wild, they dwell in murky waters filled with dense aquatic vegetation.

110 The axolotl's heart can be seen beating beneath its translucent skin, captivating observers.

111

In their natural habitat, they can be found in various types of aquatic ecosystems, from deep lakes to shallow canals.

112

Axolotls have a keen sense of proprioception, enabling them to sense the position and movement of their own bodies

113 they are sometimes called "nature's superheroes" for their extraordinary regenerative abilities.

114 they communicate with each other using subtle body movements and vibrations.

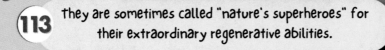

115 In Mexican folklore, axolotls are often associated with Xolotl, the god of death.

116 these amphibians are known to have a territorial side, often claiming certain areas within their tanks.

117 their primary diet consists of small aquatic invertebrates, like insects and worms.

118 Axolotls exhibit cannibalistic behavior when stressed, in crowded conditions, or when hungry.

they are often bred for their unique colors and patterns, making them popular pets.

119

120

In the wild, axolotls play an important role in maintaining the balance of their aquatic ecosystems.

these creatures display endearing behaviors such as "smiling" and "hugging" their own bodies.

121

122

Axolotls can go without food for weeks, thanks to their ability to store energy in their tails.

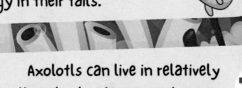

Axolotls can live in relatively small tanks, but larger enclosures are better for their well-being.

123

124 they have a unique way of making themselves appear larger by inflating their bodies with air.

125 they are sensitive to changes in temperature and should be kept within a specific range.

126 Axolotls can consume food as large as their own body thanks to their remarkable jaw flexibility.

127 they rely on their sense of smell more than their poor eyesight to locate food.

128

When males encounter each other during breeding, they engage in non-aggressive sparring to establish dominance.

129

When threatened, they can voluntarily shed their tails as a diversion tactic, allowing them to escape from predators.

130 Their sensitivity to water quality makes them ideal for teaching responsibility to young pet owners.

131 They have a variety of expressions, from curious and alert to peaceful and content.

132 They have specific breeding seasons, during which they gather to lay eggs in shallow water.

133 Axolotls are creatures of the night, most active during the evening and nighttime.

134 In ancient Mexico, axolotls were considered a delicacy and were part of traditional dishes.

135 These amphibians have a primitive lateral line system for detecting movement in the water.

If an axolotl loses a tooth, it can grow a new one to replace it. **136**

137 Axolotls can learn to associate certain sights and sounds with feeding times.

Recent studies suggest they may have the ability to navigate using Earth's magnetic field. **138**

139 these animals are often mistaken for fish due to their aquatic lifestyle.

In captivity, axolotls can form strong bonds with their owners, recognizing them over time. **140**

141 Axolotls prefer a soft substrate in their tank to prevent injury to their delicate skin.

142 the axolotl's native habitat, Xochimilco, is a UNESCO World Heritage site.

143 Axolotls exhibit playful behavior, often nipping at the ends of their own tails.

144 these creatures have a mysterious and captivating presence, making them intriguing to many people.

145

When breeding, males are known to become protective parents, guarding the eggs and sometimes the hatchlings.

146

They exhibit seasonal variations in activity levels, with periods of increased activity during breeding seasons.

147 Axolotls can have unique and individual personalities, some being more curious and outgoing than others.

148 Axolotls can show signs of happiness by wagging their tails or performing a little dance in the water.

149 Axolotls have soft, permeable skin that allows them to absorb water and oxygen directly through it.

150 Axolotls are often considered a symbol of conservation efforts to protect endangered species.

151 The presence or absence of axolotls in their habitats can be an indicator of ecosystem health.

152 These creatures can grow up to a foot in length, with some individuals reaching even larger sizes.

they have a preference for a diet of live or frozen food, as they rely on movement to stimulate their appetite.

153

154 Axolotls have intricate social behaviors, which can be observed in a group setting.

they are known to occasionally playfully nip at or "hug" their tankmates without harm.

155

156 When provided with abundant food, they can grow quickly, doubling their size in just a few months.

During the breeding season, their colors may become more vibrant and patterned to attract mates.

157

158 Females are often the dominant members of their communities, leading and defending territories.

159 In their native habitat, they share the waters with other interesting creatures like turtles and frogs.

160 Despite their regeneration abilities, axolotls can still get sick, so they need proper care.

161 Their skin is extremely sensitive and susceptible to injury, so gentle handling is crucial.

162 they have well-defined territories, and intruding into another axolotl's space can lead to territorial disputes.

163 Some axolotls have tiny whisker-like barbels near their mouths, which help them sense their surroundings.

164 In the wild, axolotls have complex interactions with their environment and other species.

165 they are sometimes called "water monsters" or "water dogs" due to their curious nature.

166 Axolotls have inspired many artists and writers with their unique characteristics.

167 Axolotl eggs are relatively large, often measuring around 1.5 to 2.5 millimeters in diameter.

168 these amphibians have a body plan well-suited for their aquatic lifestyle.

169 they have an excellent ability to adapt to changing environmental conditions.

These creatures are known to wiggle their external gills, which is both adorable and functional.

170

171

Axolotls are quite skilled at squeezing through tight spaces due to their flexible bodies.

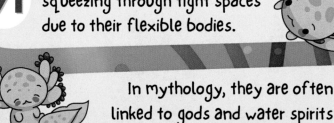

In mythology, they are often linked to gods and water spirits in various cultures.

172

173

These creatures can be born with a genetic mutation known as "gynandromorphism," where they have both male and female characteristics.

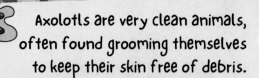

Axolotls are very clean animals, often found grooming themselves to keep their skin free of debris.

174

175 they are excellent subjects for observation and scientific experiments, given their unique characteristics.

176 the axolotl has a loyal and growing fan base worldwide, including enthusiasts and conservationists.

177 Axolotls often show curiosity by investigating objects and structures in their tanks.

178 these amphibians are a living testament to the mysteries of nature and evolution.

179

they have a highly efficient digestive system, capable of breaking down a variety of prey into easily absorbed nutrients.

180

their conservation is vital not only for the axolotls themselves but for the entire Xochimilco ecosystem.

181 Axolotls have been cherished by the indigenous peoples of Mexico for centuries.

182 Their unique appearance has made them a symbol of conservation and environmental awareness.

183 In the wild, axolotls can be elusive, making them challenging to spot.

184 they can tolerate a wide range of water pH levels, making them adaptable to different conditions.

185 Axolotls are skilled at burrowing into the substrate, providing an element of surprise to their prey.

186 they can have mottled or speckled skin patterns, adding to their individuality.

their skin is sensitive to ultraviolet light, so they should be kept out of direct sunlight.

187

188
When stressed, they can release a cloud of mucus as a defense mechanism to deter potential threats.

Axolotls have been featured in video games, creating a new generation of enthusiasts.

189

190
the incubation period for axolotl eggs varies but generally lasts around 10 to 14 days.

these creatures have been known to change their coloration in response to temperature shifts.

191

192 their regenerative capabilities have sparked hopes of one day applying the same principles to humans.

193 Although aquatic, they can tolerate brief periods on land if necessary.

194 their presence can help prevent the proliferation of aquatic pests by consuming their eggs.

195 they engage in symbiotic relationships with some fish species, where the fish eat parasites off the axolotl's skin.

196

their regenerating tails have a surprising level of control and can be manipulated to create intricate shapes.

197

When a limb is regenerating, it can appear as a small, translucent nub, gradually growing into a fully functional limb.

198 they help improve water quality by filtering small particles and debris through their gills.

199 they release chemical signals to convey messages about territory, breeding readiness, and more.

200 While they may travel in search of mates, they return to their home territory for shelter and safety.

201 In the wild, they occasionally surface to bask in the sunlight, absorbing vital nutrients.

202 They sometimes exhibit communal nesting behaviors, with multiple females using a single nest.

203 their burrows provide refuge for various aquatic species and create microhabitats within ecosystems.

Made in the USA
Las Vegas, NV
22 November 2024

11925589R00031